Las manadas de dinosaurios

por Tim Glazer
ilustrado por Burgandy Beam

Scott Foresman
is an imprint of

Glenview, Illinois • Boston, Massachusetts • Chandler, Arizona
Upper Saddle River, New Jersey

Every effort has been made to secure permission and provide appropriate credit for photographic material. The publisher deeply regrets any omission and pledges to correct errors called to its attention in subsequent editions.

Unless otherwise acknowledged, all photographs are the property of Pearson.

Illustrations by Burgandy Beam

ISBN 13: 978-0-328-53307-7
ISBN 10:   0-328-53307-6

Copyright © by Pearson Education, Inc., or its affiliates. All rights reserved. Printed in the United States of America. This publication is protected by copyright, and permission should be obtained from the publisher prior to any prohibited reproduction, storage in a retrieval system, or transmission in any form or by any means, electronic, mechanical, photocopying, recording, or likewise. For information regarding permissions, write to Pearson Curriculum Rights & Permissions, One Lake Street, Upper Saddle River, New Jersey 07458.

Pearson® is a trademark, in the U.S. and/or other countries, of Pearson plc or its affiliates.

Scott Foresman® is a trademark, in the U.S. and/or other countries, of Pearson Education, Inc., or its affiliates.

2 3 4 5 6 7 8 9 10 V0N4 13 12 11 10

Ya no hay dinosaurios en la Tierra.

Vivieron en el pasado.

Estos tres dinosaurios vivían solos.

Otros dinosaurios vivían en manadas.

En una manada hay muchos animales.

Esta manada hace un gran círculo.

Sus bebés están dentro.

Este gran dinosaurio quiere comer.

Todos en la manada se mueven juntos.

Los bebés siguen seguros allí, dentro del círculo.

Los dinosaurios de las manadas corrían y cazaban juntos.

Esta manada derrotará al dinosaurio grande.

La manada consigue su cena con él.

Los dinosaurios de las manadas hacían nidos juntos.

Esta manada hizo un nido entre los guijarros para los huevos.

Este dinosaurio grande protegía el nido.

Ya no hay dinosaurios en la Tierra.

Vivieron en el pasado.

Estos dinosaurios vivían en manadas.

El veterinario los ayuda

por Patricia Abello

ilustrado por Susan Frankenberry

Scott Foresman
is an imprint of

Glenview, Illinois • Boston, Massachusetts • Chandler, Arizona
Upper Saddle River, New Jersey

Every effort has been made to secure permission and provide appropriate credit for photographic material. The publisher deeply regrets any omission and pledges to correct errors called to its attention in subsequent editions.

Unless otherwise acknowledged, all photographs are the property of Pearson.

Photo locations denoted as follows: Top (T), Center (C), Bottom (B), Left (L), Right (R), Background (Bkgd)

Illustrations by Susan Frankenberry

Photograph 8 Digital Vision

ISBN 13: 978-0-328-53293-3
ISBN 10:   0-328-53293-2

Copyright © by Pearson Education, Inc., or its affiliates. All rights reserved. Printed in the United States of America. This publication is protected by copyright, and permission should be obtained from the publisher prior to any prohibited reproduction, storage in a retrieval system, or transmission in any form or by any means, electronic, mechanical, photocopying, recording, or likewise. For information regarding permissions, write to Pearson Curriculum Rights & Permissions, One Lake Street, Upper Saddle River, New Jersey 07458.

Pearson® is a trademark, in the U.S. and/or other countries, of Pearson plc or its affiliates.

Scott Foresman® is a trademark, in the U.S. and/or other countries, of Pearson Education, Inc., or its affiliates.

2 3 4 5 6 7 8 9 10 V0N4 13 12 11 10

¡El pajarito está herido en su nido!

David lo ve.
Él lo va a ayudar.

¡El gatito está herido!

Daniel lo ve.
Él lo va a ayudar.

¡En el veterinario cada uno está feliz!

Albergue de animales

Leamos juntos

Como muchos seres vivos, los animales necesitan albergue, comida, agua y aire. Los albergues de animales son lugares donde los animales reciben las cosas que necesitan. En algunos albergues hay veterinarios que curan a los animales enfermos o heridos.

Es bueno ayudar a los animales. Pero si encuentras un animalito perdido o herido, no debes tocarlo. Tal vez sea peligroso. Pide a un adulto conocido que te ayude. Llama a un albergue para que curen al animal.